OUR LADY OF GUADALUPE

Written by Bart Tesoriero

Illustrations: Emiguel Puod

TABLE OF CONTENTS

Library of Congress Control Number: 2011910780

ISBN 978-1-936020-27-0

Moses and the Burning Bush

One day, while Moses was tending his sheep, God appeared to him in a burning bush. Moses was surprised that the bush did not burn up, and so he went nearer to see it. God called, "Moses! Moses!" He answered "Here I am." God told Moses to come no nearer until he had removed his sandals, for he was standing on holy ground.

"I am the God of your father," God said, "the God of Abraham, Isaac, and Jacob. I have seen the affliction of my people Israel and I have come down to rescue them from the Egyptians and lead them into Canaan, a good and spacious land. I will send you to Pharaoh to lead my people out of Egypt into the Promised Land."

God promised to be with Moses to help him. He kept His promises. He delivered His people from Egypt, into the Promised Land.

We see that God can appear to His people to help them. Sometimes He sends His Mother to help us, as He has done at the shrines of Lourdes, or of Fatima. But before those other apparitions, long ago, our Mother Mary appeared in Mexico. She left the Mexican people, and all of us, a gift that is very special. She left us the gift of herself, in the image of Our Lady of Guadalupe. Let us first learn a little about Mary.

Mother Mary

God chose Mary from all women to be the Mother of His Son, Jesus. No other person has ever been so blessed. Mary was pure and filled with grace from the very first moment of her life. One day, the Angel Gabriel appeared to Mary from heaven. He said, "Behold, you will give birth to a son, and you shall call him Jesus. He will be great, and he will be called the Son of the Most High God." Mary said, "Let it be done unto me according to your word."

Mary cared for Jesus with all the love in her heart, just like your mother cares for you. One day, Jesus and His friends went to a wedding. Mary was there too. When she saw that there was no more wine to drink, Mary told Jesus, "They have no wine." To the servers she said, "Do whatever he tells you." Jesus changed water into wine.

From the cross, Jesus gave Mary to His beloved apostle, John. Then Jesus gave John to His mother Mary. She felt the same tender love she had felt when Jesus was a baby. Like God the Father, Mary gave her only son so that we might be saved from sin and live a new life. When her life was over, Mary was taken up body and soul into heaven. From heaven, she continues to comfort and console all of her children. Jesus crowned Mary as Queen of heaven and earth, Queen of all the angels and saints! Mary is our Mother in heaven. She loves all her children!

The Conquest of Mexico

Long ago, the Aztec Indians ruled Mexico and much of Central America. In the year 1503 they chose Montezuma to be their king. He ruled from an island in Lake Texcoco called Mexico City, home of the people called the Mexica. Montezuma captured many Indians from other tribes. He made them give many gifts and much gold to the Aztecs. He also sacrificed many of them to the Aztec gods.

On Good Friday, 1519, a Spanish conquistador named Hernando Cortez landed on the Gulf shore of Mexico with soldiers and horses. He made friends with some of the Indians there. They joined his small army and together they began to move toward Mexico City. Some of the Indians they met along the way fought Cortez and his soldiers. After a great struggle, Cortez and his men won these battles, and the Indians joined him.

In November, 1519, Cortez and his soldiers entered Mexico City. At first, Montezuma welcomed Cortez, whom he thought was a god. He gave him flowers and fruit and many gifts. Later, the Aztecs fought the Spaniards. After many months, Cortez and his men defeated the Aztecs and stopped the sacrifices to their gods. They tried to teach the people about Jesus and the Catholic faith, but most of the Aztecs did not believe.

Juan Diego

Juan Diego was an Aztec Indian born in 1474. His name in Aztec was "Singing Eagle." He was very poor. His parents died when he was young. Juan's uncle helped to raise him. When Juan Diego became an adult, he married a woman named Malitzin. He and his wife lived near his uncle. Juan Diego worked in the fields and made mats.

Sometime around 1523, Franciscan priests from Spain preached to the Aztecs about Jesus and the Catholic Faith. Juan Diego, his wife, and his uncle believed the Gospel. They walked 30 miles to the church in Mexico City for Mass and instructions in the Faith. They accepted Jesus as their Savior and were baptized in the year 1525. Their Baptismal names were Juan Diego, Maria Lucia (his wife) and Juan Bernardino (his uncle).

Sadly, Juan Diego's wife died in 1529. Since they had no children, Juan went to live near his uncle. Juan Diego cared for him, for Juan Bernardino had became very sick.

The Franciscan priests offered Holy Mass on Saturdays in honor of Our Lady at the church of Santiago (Saint James) in the nearby town. Juan ran the 7 miles from his village to the church so as not to be late for Mass.

Juan Diego Sees a Beautiful Lady

On Saturday morning, December 9th, 1531, Juan Diego awoke early for Mass as usual. As he ran up a small hill called Tepeyac, Juan heard the sweet shrill song of birds chirping at the first light of dawn. Suddenly their song ended. Juan stopped, amazed. Then from the top of the hill, he heard the voice of a young woman, calling his name: "Juanito!"

Juan climbed to the top of the hill. As he looked up, he saw rays like the sun beaming brightly around the head and feet of a young Indian girl. She was about 16 years old and so very beautiful! She wore a blue cape covered in stars. The lovely lady appeared to be an Aztec princess. He waited, and she spoke. "Juan, smallest and dearest of my little children, where are you going?"

Juan replied, "I was hurrying to Mass." The woman said, "Dear little son, I love you. I am the ever-Virgin Mary, Mother of the true God who gives life." Juan fell to his knees. The beautiful lady continued, "God made everything and He is in all places. He is the Lord of heaven and earth. I desire a temple, a church, in this place where I will show my love to your people. I want to show my compassion to all people who ask my help. Here I will see their tears. I will console them and they will be at ease. Run now to tell the bishop all you have seen and heard."

The Lady Appears Again

Juan Diego ran as fast as he could to Mexico City. He felt some fear, because the Spanish soldiers were sometimes mean to the Indians. However, he remembered the beautiful Lady, and felt strong in his heart. Finally he arrived at the palace of Bishop Zumarraga. The servants made Juan wait, but finally brought him to the bishop.

Juan told Bishop Zumarraga all about the Lady and her request for a church. The bishop listened kindly to Juan. Then he dismissed Juan, saying he would think about his request. That night, Juan slowly made his way back home, tired and sad that the bishop did not believe him. As he passed the hill of Tepeyac, suddenly the beautiful Lady appeared to him again! "Listen, my little son," she said. "I have chosen you for this task. Tomorrow go to see the bishop again and tell him the Virgin Mary greatly desires for him to build a church in this place."

The next morning, Sunday, December 10th, Juan returned to Mexico City. Bishop Zumarraga was surprised to see him again so soon, but he listened patiently to Juan. He told Juan to ask the Lady for a sign. Juan left the palace and ran back to the hill. He knelt before Our Lady and told her of the bishop's request. She said, "Very well, my little son. Come back tomorrow and I will give you a sign."

Mary Gives a Sign

Juan went home and found that his uncle was very sick. Juan cared for him all that night and the next day, Monday, as well. He did not go to see the Lady. Juan feared that his uncle was dying. Early Tuesday morning, December 12th, Juan left his uncle to go bring the priest. As Juan Diego ran past the hill of Tepeyac, the Blessed Mother appeared to him again.

"My little son," she said, "do not be afraid. Am I not here who am your Mother? Are you not under my protection? Your uncle will not die. At this very moment he is cured."

Juan felt a deep peace in his heart. Mary told him to climb the hill and cut the flowers growing there. Juan knew that no flowers ever grew in the cold winter, as the ground was frozen. Still, he obeyed Mary, and climbed the hill. There, before him, were beautiful roses such as only grew in Spain! Juan cut them and put them in his tilma, which was like a cape worn in front of him. Then he ran down to the Lady. Mary arranged the roses tenderly with her own hands, and then tied the tilma in back of Juan so that no flowers would drop out. She told him to return to the bishop. "Do not let anyone but the bishop see what you are carrying. Tell him everything you have seen and heard this morning. This time he will believe you."

An Amazing Miracle!

As Juan Diego made his way along the mountains back to the city of Mexico, he enjoyed the sweet perfume of the roses he carried. When he arrived at the bishop's palace, the servants pulled at his tilma, trying to see the flowers, but Juan held on tightly. He remembered Our Lady's words to him. "I must show the roses only to the bishop!" he said. Finally the servants allowed Juan Diego to enter into the bishop's room.

Juan Diego stood in front of the Bishop Zumarraga and his servants. He told the bishop everything the Blessed Mother had told him to say. Then, Juan reached up and untied his tilma. His cloak fell open before the Bishop, and the roses tumbled out at his feet. The bishop fell to his knees in amazement, as did his servants. They pointed to Juan's tilma in awe. Juan looked down in front of him. To his wonder he saw the Virgin herself, imprinted on his tilma!

The bishop and his servants spent some time in holy silence and prayer before the image. Then the bishop slowly arose and gently untied the tilma from around Juan's neck. He carried it into his private chapel, and hung it on the wall. There, Juan Diego knelt with the others in prayerful wonder at this most amazing miracle of God's love. The Mother of Jesus had come to stay!

The Image of Our Lady

The Aztec Indians used pictures as part of their language. Therefore the image of Our Lady spoke to them in a very special way. The Lady stood in front of the sun, with its rays shining behind her. This meant she was greater than the sun-god of the Aztecs. She stood on the moon, which meant she had triumphed over the moon-god. Her cloak was a blue-green, which meant she was a Queen. The stars on her cloak told them she was greater than the stars which they worshipped.

The Lady's hands were folded in prayer and her head was bowed. This told the Aztecs that she was not a god, but was honoring the true God who was greater than her. She wore a tiny black cross on a gold medal around her neck. This meant she was the same religion as the Spanish conquerors. Her rose-colored dress reminded them of the dawn as the sun rose to give new life.

The Lady's face was so very kind and full of compassion. Mary was standing on the head of a snake, which meant she had crushed the devil. The black band around her waist was a sign that she was pregnant, and carrying a baby in her womb. It also meant she was offering this baby to them and to all the peoples of the New World. A tiny flower was placed over her womb, a sign of her holy Child.

A Church for Our Lady

The next morning Bishop Zumarraga and his priests carried the tilma of Juan Diego in procession to the cathedral. The news of the miraculous image and message of the Lady was already spreading quickly throughout Mexico City.

Juan showed the bishop the hill of Tepeyac, where the Virgin Mary had requested that a church be built. Juan then returned to his uncle. His uncle told Juan that as he lay dying, a beautiful lady had appeared to him in a gentle glow of light. She told him he would recover from his illness. She also said that she had sent his nephew with a picture of herself to the bishop. "Call me and my image Santa Maria of Guadalupe," she said, and then she vanished. "Guadalupe" was the name of a shrine of Mary in Spain. However, it also sounds like the Aztec word for "She who crushes the serpent."

The Indians helped Bishop Zumarraga build a small church on the hill of Tepeyac. He also built a little chapel nearby for Juan Diego. Many people came to see the miracle and to pray before the image of the beautiful Lady. Juan Diego told his fellow Aztecs and the other Indians the story of Our Lady of Guadalupe and urged them to accept Jesus and the Catholic Faith.

The Indians Accept Jesus and Mary

As the story of Our Lady of Guadalupe spread, many more
Indians and Spaniards came to see and visit the shrine. The
Indians especially were moved by the love of this Mother who
looked like them and spoke their language. She had appeared
to one of their own people, an Aztec! The Virgin Mary had
come to them on the hill of Tepeyac, which had been the hill
of their mother-god.

Juan Diego explained that Mary was the Mother of the true
God. Her religion, the religion of Christianity, was to replace
their Aztec religion. The natives listened to the good news of
Jesus and the Gospel. They learned that God had sent his only
Son to die for all people. His one sacrifice saved them all. They
did not need to sacrifice to their god any more. Many of the
Indians believed and were baptized, sometimes thousands of
them in a single day! They realized that God loved them as
much as He loved the Spaniards from across the sea.

As the Catholic Faith spread, the people began to yearn for a
new life, a life that was pure and good. They wanted to be
children of this Mother who had come to them. They wanted
to learn about her Son, who was, as she had said, the true
God. They found out that He wanted them to live forever
with Him and His Mother in heaven.

The Patroness of Mexico

In the next few years, 8 million Indians were baptized! After they were baptized, the people learned about Jesus and Mary and their new faith. Many of them married the Spaniards, and the Mexican people came to be a new community.

Bishop Zumarraga built a little home for Juan Diego, called a hermitage, next to the chapel at Tepeyac. Juan Diego lived there, telling the story of Our Lady and of the miraculous image to the many pilgrims who visited the shrine. Juan Diego died in peace on May 30, 1548. He was buried at Tepeyac. Three days later Bishop Zumarraga died as well.

In 1709, the first Basilica of Our Lady of Guadalupe was built. It was one of the most beautiful churches in the Americas. The image of Our Lady was installed above the altar. All people were welcome to come and venerate the image and pray to Our Lady. In 1895, Pope Leo told the Bishop of Mexico City to crown the image of Our Lady of Guadalupe. Fifty years later, in 1945, Pope Pius proclaimed our Lady of Guadalupe as the Patroness of all the Americas. In 1976, a new basilica was dedicated. It holds 10,000 people! Each year 10 million people visit the Basilica of Our Lady of Guadalupe. It is the most popular shrine of Our Blessed Mother Mary in the whole world!

Blessed John Paul II
and Our Lady of Guadalupe

Pope John Paul II had a great devotion to Our Lady of Guadalupe. The people of Mexico were also very dear to him. In 1979, one year after his election, Pope John Paul II visited the shrine of Our Lady of Guadalupe. He visited the shrine in Mexico City again in 1990. At that time he "beatified" Juan Diego, declaring him to be Blessed. The pope said that Blessed Juan Diego was the greatest evangelist of all times.

In 1999 Pope John Paul visited the basilica of Our Lady of Guadalupe a third time. He declared that her feast day, December 12th, was to be celebrated as a holy day for the whole continent of America. He also entrusted all children to Mary's motherly care, especially all unborn children still in the wombs of their mothers.

In 2002, Pope John Paul made his final visit to Mexico. At that time, he canonized Saint Juan Diego. His feast day is December 9th, the date he first saw Our Lady on the hill of Tepeyac. Pope John Paul honored Saint Juan Diego for his simple faith and trust in God. Juan Diego had told the Virgin Mary that he was a "small rope or a tiny ladder," but he allowed God to use him to bring Jesus to many, many people.

Prayer to Our Lady of Guadalupe

Our Lady of Guadalupe loves you and your family too. Here is a prayer you can pray every day to Our Lady. Ask her to pray with you and for you to her Son, Jesus.

Memorare Prayer to Our Lady of Guadalupe
by Pope John Paul II
(Abridged)

Remember, O most gracious Virgin Mary of Guadalupe, that on Mount Tepeyac, you promised to show pity and compassion to all who seek your help and protection. You promised to listen to our prayers, to dry our tears, and to give us consolation. Never was it known that anyone who fled to your protection, implored your help, or sought your intercession, was left unaided.

Inspired with this confidence, we fly unto you, O Mary, ever Virgin Mother of the True God! We kneel before you, in your presence, certain that you will fulfill your merciful promises. We are full of hope that, standing beneath your shadow and protection, nothing will trouble or afflict us. We do not need to be afraid, for you have decided to remain with us in a special way through your image. O Holy Mother of God, in your mercy hear and answer us. Amen.

Prayer to Saint Juan Diego

Dear Saint Juan Diego, we honor you today. At the hill of Tepeyac our Lady told you, "I am your Mother. Are you not under my protection? Why do you fear, if you are in my mantle, and in my arms?" In your humility, you were necessary in God's plan.

You faced Bishop Zumarraga with courage. You presented him with the miracle of roses which grew on the hillside. In a wonderful way, the image of the Virgin Mary appeared on your tilma!

Because of your faithfulness, dear Saint Juan Diego, the Gospel of our Lord Jesus Christ spread through Mary's image. Many people came to believe in Him. Your devotion lives on in the people of Mexico, in the people of North and South America, and the whole world.

O Saint Juan Diego, please pray for us. (*Ask what you would like God to do for you and for your family.*)

May Our Lady of Guadalupe, Mother of the true God, bring all people to Jesus, her Son. Dear God, we ask all this of You, through Christ our Lord. Amen.

The Words of Our Lady to Juan Diego

"My dear little Juan Diego. Listen and let my words enter your heart. Let not your heart be disturbed. Do not fear any sickness or sorrow. Am I not here, who am your Mother? Are you not under my shadow and protection? Am I not your health?

"Am I not your fountain of life? Are you not happily within my folds of my mantle? Are you not cuddled in the crossing of my arms? Is there anything else you need? Do not grieve nor be disturbed by anything."

Our Lady of Guadalupe, pray for us!
Saint Juan Diego, pray for us!